MANGA LIFE

FIND
TRUE LOVE

LISA HELMANIS, SABINA DOSANI AND PETER CROSS
WITH ILLUSTRATIONS BY SONIA LEONG

Brilliant ideas

Introduction

Who would have thought that something as simple and natural as meeting and keeping a partner would need a manual? After all, it's easy. Don't your eyes just meet across a crowded room, then you make idle chatter and impress each other with your witty repartee, and the next thing you know it's all mini-breaks, expensive dinners with flattering low lighting and happily ever after? Right?

Wrong. Our expectations of love, romance and sex have altered massively since only a generation ago: now statistics show that almost half of all marriages end in divorce. We're all working longer hours, and add to that the high cost of living, and – well, you get the picture. Romance gets moved to the back burner. So how do you avoid becoming a statistic? Hopefully the tips in this book will go a long way to helping you.

If you're in a relationship, or trying to find your mate, this book's for you. You don't have to be married, straight, or over 25. Nor do you have to wait until you and your relationship have become jaded and tired before trying these brilliant ideas. On the contrary, the earlier you sit down and think about your life together the better.

We don't promise to stop arguments forever, or guarantee that you'll never feel angry with each other again. This is real life. We are here to promote possibilities, not pipe dreams. Forget rules, you need ideas. So what are you waiting for?

I'M KEN AND I'M A FASHION MODEL. AND THIS HERE IS PETE.
ECONOMICS LECTURER. WE'RE OLD FRIENDS FROM SCHOOL.
AND WE ARE ALL HOUSEMATES!
THIS BOOK IS CALLED "FIND TRUE LOVE" AND IT'S ALL ABOUT ROMANCE AND RELATIONSHIPS.
HMM... I COULD REALLY DO WITH HELP ON THIS... I'M ALWAYS GETTING THE WRONG TYPE OF GUY, OR THINGS JUST DON'T WORK OUT...

MY PROBLEM IS THAT I CAN'T CHOOSE – SO MANY GUYS, SO LITTLE TIME... AND I LIKE THEM ALL!

I'M VERY SHY, I HAVEN'T HAD MANY GIRLFRIENDS... I WOULD LIKE TO MEET SOMEONE THOUGH...

AND I HAVE A LONG TERM PARTNER, LISA. WE'VE BEEN TOGETHER FOR A FEW YEARS.

Hi!

WE HOPE THAT YOU ENJOY OUR ADVENTURES IN FINDING TRUE LOVE!

1. Learn from the masters

*Everyone knows someone who is an incredible flirt
– now it's your turn…*

Flirting doesn't have to be about sex. It can just be about remembering to look up, crack a smile and not take everything so seriously. Most good flirts have a few skills in common. Firstly, they smile a lot. They just keep things upbeat, a quality that draws people whether they are friends or colleagues. Secondly, they ask questions and remember details. And thirdly, they often use physical contact. Touching their arm or hand as you chat, taking their elbow as you go through a door – these are all ways of making people know that you are comfortable with the idea of being in their body space: or of having them in yours.

This is why you also need to think about how you already put yourself out there. Are you always coming up with wisecracks or reminding men you meet how smart you are? Do you find yourself joking about, like one of the lads? Whilst this might be a great place to get to with a partner, it's not necessarily ideal when you first meet someone.

You can also use what the flirt does wrong to help guide you: maybe her whole conversation is about the other person, which is a great way to get attention but isn't going to help move things on to the next stage. Maybe the neckline of her blouse ends around her waistband; also not a winner with every guy in town.

2. Facing the facts

The key skill to learn when mastering the art of dating
is the art of truth.

You will find yourself suffering unnecessarily during the whole dating process if you cannot face a few facts (and hide some). Men aren't that complex. If they want you, they will find you. If it has taken him more than around five days to call, then one of the following statements is probably true:

- He isn't that into you, but wants some entertainment.
- He has a girlfriend and couldn't get to the phone till she went off to visit her mum.
- He thinks he is a player, and someone told him playing hard to get would drive you insane. (Note; this is also sometimes known as mental abuse.)
- He is incapable of/not ready for/frightened of a relationship.
- He genuinely lost your number and has had to track you down through Interpol, so desperate was he to see you.

Of course, you may feel the need to see him again to work out which one of the above is at play. And if it's any of them, bar Interpol, make sure you attend the date with running shoes on. Because if it is any of the above, you are better off facing a slightly unpleasant truth with a side order of disappointment, which may take a day to get over, than wait a few months down the line till your confidence and belief in men have both taken a beating.

3. Why men love bitches

...and lovely women put up with creeps.

Most men need some bitchiness. The bitch will do the routine domestic chores but will also make sure - as her partner would - that it takes effort and that he or she expects appreciation in exchange for doing them.

The key quality a bitch needs to adopt in practice is the ability to say no. If you don't want to do something, don't go and do it and then seethe in quiet resentment. It makes you feel uncomfortable and him want to avoid you like the plague. So just get it out.

Something many women fear is being regarded as high maintenance - but does anyone really wanted to be regarded as low maintenance? If you are clear about your needs and communicate them in a pleasant, unemotional way you stand a better chance of getting what you want. Saying 'Seven is too early to meet this evening for me, eight is better,' will let him know that you have a life and are not so desperate for attention that you will drop everything for his.

You might see missing your lunch hour so you can finish your work early and make the date on time as being helpful, but he will see it as being needy. And the more he pulls away the more tempting it is to try and please him. Not a great power balance to set up in the early days.

4. Message in a bottle

Alcohol, the great lifter of spirits, calmer of nerves and friend of the good times. If only that was all it did...

While alcohol has its virtues, it can also cause a whole big heap of trouble. While alcohol may make it possible for you to say a full sentence without stuttering when you're on a date, it may also mean that the sentence is a rather intimate list of all the embarrassing men you've ever slept with.

There are a few great tricks to make sure that you don't end up drinking yourself into a stupor on your date. Firstly, make sure that you order water as well as wine with dinner and take alternate sips. This will help with your hangover as well as your clarity. Secondly, if you are meeting for cocktails, resist the urge to order a martini and go for something a little more sedate; a longer drink, mixed with fruit juice or soda, can pack a punch but also keep you this side of bursting into Cole Porter classics. If you are going speed dating or to a party, then make sure that you don't arrive too early, otherwise you are bound to start drinking to calm your nerves.

When you start to feel like your judgement is going, get a cab. If you like each other you can get together again; if not you will be glad you woke up in your own bed (alone). And if it is just some nice casual maintenance sex you are after, wouldn't it be better to be able to remember it?

5. Money
– the sticky stuff

*Modern dating's a confusing world, not least because many
women are independent, don't need escorts to be allowed out
and can afford to buy their own handbags.*

So, as well as the old-fashioned rules about who asks who out, we also have the thorny issue of who picks up the bill... As a rule of thumb, whoever asks for the date should be the one to pay. However, money is not neutral and you need to think about what kind of message you are sending out when you make your decision. Many men feel uncomfortable if a woman wants to pay; it's their last vestige of masculinity when it comes to feeling like a provider (don't laugh, it's an important part of a normal man's identity).

However, you may have fallen for a fledgling photographer who has yet to make any money, while you are riding high on your expense account. So try a picnic in the park or trips to a gallery that he can stump up for, or he will get tired of being the poor relation

and move on. There is no denying that money is power and must be handled with care to stop it causing rifts.

Money is an emotional issue and cited as one of the key issues in a relationship breakdowns. Getting these thorny issues upfront could save you both a lot of hurt later. Money is often a great way of working out where you are at in many ways: think about how it informs your emotional decisions.

6. Live sexy

Picture the scene: you are having lunch by yourself in a quiet café; you look up and see two attractive men at nearby tables.

Both are nice looking and have good bodies, and both keep looking at you... The first, with unkempt hair has hunched shoulders and looks furtive. The second sits back in the chair and waits for you to look up before giving you a wide smile and then looking back to his menu. Which one appeals?

A person who seems in a happy, self-possessed place is always going to be more of a draw than anybody who looks like they need to be put through a spin cycle on extra hot. And it's not all about body language; it's about the fact that we would all like to be with someone who can enrich our lives rather than drain them.

Here are five easy ways to make your life utterly desirable.

* Act like you know your own worth, no matter how you feel.
* Hang on to your friends – no one wants a limpet relying on them for constant love and stimulus.
* Get smart with money – a very attractive quality to others, it will give you a great sense of well-being and security too.
* Take some pride in your living environment and you'll appear more sorted and feel more relaxed.
* Make sure you maintain your other interests after you start dating.

7. Make anyone want you

Using a few tricks to get someone interested isn't just a cynical ploy. Real love will follow if it's right.

Mirroring is a technique that has been observed by psychologists in happy couples, in fact it seems to be essential to their happiness. The great news is that if you are looking to make an impact on someone, you can use this technique from the very start, in the form of sexy body language; touching your face if they touch theirs, leaning forward if they do… it seems to be a natural instinct that we can lose as relationships evolve and we get defensive.

Repeat back ideas or phrases that they use, or make comments such as 'I can understand why you feel frustrated' or 'I really sympathise with that'. This will make them feel as if you share a common bond and world view, something essential to falling in love.

There is a difference between mirroring someone's behaviour and becoming a strange, puppet-like version of them. You can still disagree with them and take a different stance on things, but allow someone to feel understood before you get into that sticky place where you disagree (which we are all bound to do at times). If you have been together for a little while, and feel that things quickly seem to jump to a state of friction between the two of you, then try getting back to a place of complicity by employing this technique.

IS THAT THE NEW PHD STUDENT I'M SHOWING AROUND?

SHE'S GORGEOUS!!

BETTER MAKE A GOOD IMPRESSION... WHAT DID KEN TELL ME?

DR. LEWIS?

OH, PLEASE CALL ME PETE!

"MIRROR HER BODY LANGUAGE" OR SOMETHING LIKE THAT?

JULIE, IS IT?

JULIE KENT. FIRST TIME ON CAMPUS FOR ME.

AH, I'M A NEW LECTURER MYSELF.

YOU OUGHT TO PICK UP A HOBBY OR JOIN A CLUB TO MEET OTHER STUDENTS.

I JOINED THE EROTIC FILM SOCIETY YESTERDAY.

...

SO WHAT DO YOU DO IN YOUR SPARE TIME? LET ME GUESS...

...

YOU'RE A MIME AT KIDS PARTIES?

8. And what do you do?

Upgrade your small talk and a better grade romance becomes a lot more likely.

Instead of being bored to death by yet another conversation about commuting or the weather, suggest something you're interested in and most other people are, too. Sex if it's the right sort of environment. Travel or scandal if you want to be a mite more sedate. Conversation is a little bit like sport, you will play to the level you are in. If someone is deadly dull, you're more likely to be so yourself and dull is NOT sexy. Either walk away from them or try to change the subject matter. Most people are just as keen as you are to enjoy life. They will also want to sparkle and a good conversation will help them do that.

Most people like to talk about themselves and have something interesting to say, even if it's not immediately apparent. In other words, you need to bring this something interesting out of them and use the time with them to bring out their best side.

When somebody starts a dull conversation try to respond in a playful or slightly off the wall way to keep them on their toes. Of course, some days the original one-liners will just flow. On others you'll feel totally stuck and unable even to tell someone what time it is. Concentrate a bit harder to come across as sexy and amusing. Make an effort, and once you start entertaining yourself your mood will change.

9. Work it

How to look sensual after a hard day at work.

When there is no time to go home in between work and play the first thing to do is prepare. The night before go to bed early, having had a long bath and done any essential grooming such as leg waxing, manicure, eyebrow plucking...

Make sure you have at least an hour between work and the date. This time needs to be used to give you that 'just left the bathroom' look and feel. If you don't feel like lugging a whole new wardrobe to work with you just take another shirt or top and shoes with you – the right choice can transform office wear to evening wear.

Once you have finished your high-powered day, arm yourself with your make-up bag and evening clothes and lock yourself in the office loo. Remove day make-up and immediately apply your moisturiser. Then wash under your arms; if you can, also wash your feet. Then put to good use all the kit you've brought with you.

Now shake away the office from your brain as well as your body. Stand up straight, reach your arms above your head and then breathe out as you reach for your toes. Breathe in once you're down there and clasp your ankles. Slowly breathe in as you bend your knees and breathe out as you straighten them, edging closer to the floor with each breath. Repeat this ten times and you're good to go.

10. In the mood for music

Music can enhance or change your feelings in a heartbeat.

" If music be the food of love, play on", said the playwright. And since time began music has been a great aphrodisiac. What music do you choose to set the mood? Classical music is classy and passionate. A most seductive piece of operatic music is the aria from Don Giovanni where he seduces Elvira. It has a flow and a pace that makes you want to fall into bed. But be careful, if you end up smooching to this you might get a rude awakening when the earth opens and Hell claims the evil seducer at the end, rather loudly. A more relaxing option might be Mozart's Clarinet Concerto; flowing, seductive, entrancing.

You could always invite your partner to dance to some slow and sexy music. Don't be self-conscious about it, just dim the lights, move the furniture out of the way, put on your favourite tune and go for it. Better still strip (or strip them) to something seductive. If you find it too embarrassing to strip and get all self conscious try loosening your inhibitions with a drink beforehand. But not too much, there's nothing as ungainly as a drunk stripper falling over her stilettos as she tries to ease off a stocking. Let the mood and the music relax and seduce you. Remember that the key to being sexy is confidence. You know you can do it. Get in touch with your inner tramp.

11. Enduring allure

What can you do to re-ignite the early relationship sparks?

It's not difficult to feel sexy at the beginning of a relationship. Just the touch of his or her hand will give you goose bumps. But sadly that sort of intensity goes with time and with familiarity.

If you possibly can then go away together alone at least once every three months or so. It's not just the fact of being alone that's important, it's being away from all the chores and worries of home. Some couples also find that making a date with each other once a week helps to keep the relationship fires burning. It's a good idea if you find it hard to prioritise each other. Decide to leave work early and meet for a drink on your way home, or meet for lunch.

Try to think of sex as a priority and make time for it. Slip into something sexy and buy your loved one a little gift and put every effort into seducing your partner. What could be more important than that? Make sure you take time to relax - you're going to find it very hard to get in the mood if you're still stressed from today or worrying about tomorrow. Add spark to your life by thinking of each day as a day filled with sexy opportunities. For example, don't just think of the bathroom as a place to shave or shower but a place to rekindle your romance. And make sure you keep yourself interesting for your partner as well as looking good.

12. No place like home

Going out on dates can only be sustained for so long. The real romance happens at home.

Even if you're living together you should regularly create a sexy environment at home. It's a lot cheaper than going out, and you can get naked a lot quicker. Once you are alone use the time wisely and don't waste it dealing with mundane tasks such as bills.

Choose mellow, romantic music and soften the lighting by turning down the lights or just using candles – magical. (But just make sure you don't inadvertently create any fire hazards). Floating candles create a flattering and sensual light. Make sure the room smells sensual by burning some fragranced oils for a few minutes. This will give you a much more subtle and natural aroma than you would get by spraying air freshener.

Food is going to play a large part in your sexy evening in. Pick on things you can feed each other, smear on one another or generally get dirty with. Finger food works well. Artichokes with melted butter, strawberries and whipped cream, grapes (seedless if possible, spitting out seeds is not a good look). Pink champagne is especially effective. There is something incredibly sexy and decadent about it especially when combined with strawberries.

Why not settle down together to a sexy DVD? Pick one of your old favourites or go for something unknown with a sexy element to inspire and titillate you. What comes next is entirely up to you.

13. The art of sexy travel

Getting there in style makes a big difference to how you feel once you arrive.

If you don't want to step off the plane at the start of your romantic weekend away looking like something the cat dragged in and feeling even worse there are several ways to lessen the pain.

If you are on a long-haul flight and the lights are out, put on a moisturising face pack for the night. In the morning, wash it off and put on a moisturising serum to brighten your face up. Take lots of hand cream and some of your favourite scent to spray on when you land. Don't forget your hairbrush and breath freshener too. Changing your underwear just before you land as well as your top will make you feel fresher. And remember not to succumb to the temptations of that glass of wine or gin and tonic (no matter how bored you get). Flying dehydrates you and alcohol makes it worse. Try to eat healthily, even if it means going on board with your own picnic. And remember linen is not a good option when travelling, you will arrive looking like you need a good iron.

Try to stay zen and don't get cross if there are delays or complications. These things are beyond our control, there's no point fighting them. Train travel is often a lot more relaxing, so if it's a relatively short journey why not avoid the airport all together?

14. Write away

Expressing yourself in writing is one way to keep in touch with a loved one when you're away, and can be extremely sexy.

Now that we live in the age of emails and mobile phones, the simple old letter doesn't really figure much. But it's amazing how romantic it is. Next time you're away from your loved one, try writing a letter, saying how much you miss them and describing what you would like to be doing if you were with them. The fact that someone has made the effort to write you a letter in this age of rapid communications is pretty sexy in itself. Just say what you want. You may not think it's important but your loved one will. Imagine he or she is standing in front of you and say what comes into your head. But thoughts about them will naturally interest them most. If you're planning a sexy letter use beautiful paper and, women, spray a little of your favourite scent on to remind him of you.

Emails are a great way to keep in touch. You can flirt in emails as the exchange is almost immediate, like a conversation. Send your loved one a romantic email just to say you miss them - even if you're going to see them that night.

Telephone sex is a great way to talk your lover through how much you're missing them and what you'd like to do with them. It is guaranteed to keep the sparks flying while you're away. You'll both be looking forward to the reunion more than ever.

15. Surprise!

Use a little imagination to spice up your everyday life and create romantic situations where you normally wouldn't.

Try to treat each day as an adventure. It's a terrible old cliché but live each day as if it were your last. Instead of thinking, "God this is dreadful, I hate this commute" think, "I wonder what or who is waiting around the corner?" Even if you're not optimistic anything remotely exciting awaits you on the 7.47 take something exciting with you like a novel full of steamy sex and adventure – it will at least get the imagination of your fellow commuters going.

Adopt the same approach in your relationship. try some interesting and eccentric dates. Things like ice skating or a picnic in a boat work better than a classic dinner out.

For your girlfriend's next birthday how about booking her a day at a fabulous spa with one of her friends? If she's more practical then what about a fabulous cookery course? And for your boyfriend, you really can't go wrong by giving him one of his sexual fantasies as a present (though a cookery course might work for him too).

To inject some spontaneity why not get on a bargain flight to a city you've never visited or spend all day in bed feeding each other strawberries? Whatever you do, increase the sexiness and excitement of being together by doing something you don't normally do.

OH PETE... GOT A SURPRISE FOR YOU.

WHAT IS IT?

HOLY COW!! RIBBONS AND STOCKINGS!! BEST SURPRISE EVER!!!

OH, MY LINGERIE? I WEAR THIS STUFF ALL THE TIME.

NO...

THIS IS THE SURPRISE!

OHOHOHOHO!

YOU WILL CALL ME LADY JULIE!!

16. Je ne sais quoi

The French invented romance – so what can we learn from them?

The French work at being romantic. Romance is usually on their minds. And that's very seductive. They are naturally confident (some would even say superior or snotty). So you need to think French, instil yourself with inner confidence and assurance. You are sexy, let no one tell you otherwise.

As a rule, French women are chic and elegant. Good make up and hair are essential if you're a woman, and you guys need to practice good grooming too. The fundamental mantra for the French is 'natural but not casual'. Ladies, this means light lip glosses, subtle highlights and not much eye make up. Get your eyelashes curled and dyed – you'll look better first thing in the morning. Men, don't feel embarrassed about buying male beauty products; French men having been moisturising for years. Regular hair cuts, well cut clothes, and refusal to give into middle aged spread, will do a lot to keep your partner feeling romantic.

If you're about as French as a Lancashire hotpot, fear not, this je ne sais quoi is all about attitude. Develop a more French outlook and you'll feel like you're strolling along the Croisette in Cannes not just Chorley High Street. Take up the language as well, that way you can seduce your lover in your new not-quite-native tongue.

17. Creating a romance lair

We spend over a third of our lifetimes in bed, and if we're lucky, we get to share a nice portion of that time with someone else.

But the chances of that are greatly reduced if we bring them home to reveal a stained mattress on the floor along with an unwashed duvet and a pile of pizza boxes, so apply some thought and make your bedroom beautiful. A bedroom, space permitting, should be purely for sleeping, romancin' and reclining. Watching TV, playing video games (you'd be surprised) and working should be taken elsewhere.

Avoid over-stimulating colours such as bright orange or red. Yellow-based whites, indulgent mocha or a sweet pale violet are all guaranteed to calm the soul. A messy bedroom will not say nice things about you so remember to keep it clean and tidy ·

Natural fibres are the best bedding option: they regulate the body temperature, take moisture away from the skin (should your nocturnal activities make you a little hot and bothered) and last far longer than man-made fibres. The luxury version for duvets is Siberian goose down but any feather ranges will give great comfort. For that boutique hotel level of luxury, look out for high thread count bed linen (never less than 200).

When buying a bed, bear in mind that we move around sixty times a night (and that's just sleeping) and a standard double bed gives you less sleeping width per person than a single bed! A king-size bed will give you a lot more room to play with...

18. Search for the hero

We know the score. You fell in love with somebody amazing and now your relationship isn't as wonderful as when you first met.

D o you miss the good old days, when your lover treated you like the sexiest creature on earth and made you feel warm and fuzzy? In the drudgery of our daily grind it might feel as if the hero or heroine you fell in love with has disappeared, leaving behind something less exciting. But the hero is still there, waiting in the wings to be rediscovered and nurtured back to health. It takes a bit of effort to root out your partner's inner hero. So find half an hour to yourself, grab a sheet of paper and answer the following questions:

* Why do I love my partner?
* What would I miss if we weren't together?

The tricky part is to then share your answers with your partner. Try making a comment like, 'I like it when you make me laugh. Nobody makes me laugh like you do.'

Everyone, your partner included, lives up or down to others' expectations. Try to avoid labelling your partner. If you think 'he's not romantic' or 'she's always late', you're less likely to notice the times when he does buy roses or when she arrives ahead of you. If you make a big deal of the good things he or she does they'll feel like a hero inside and be more likely to act like one.

19. A walk on the wild side

A walk is an escape from domesticity and a chance to reconnect with the person who matters.

Chances are you'll walk out with a problem and home with a solution. Unless you live in an offshore lighthouse, there is always somewhere to walk. The sort of journey we're talking about does not need to have a specific purpose or destination, though it might involve the collection of a newspaper or be broken up by a pint in a local pub; the real reason is to have a change of environment and a change of air.

Open spaces have mind-expanding properties which help you to think more clearly; all of a sudden, difficulties become more doable and problems less problematic. Walking boosts your level of serotonin, the feel-good chemical in our brains. It also releases the body's natural opiates, endorphins, giving you a buzz. When we walk with our partner we associate feeling high with him or her.

Walks give couples a chance to talk and think. And on warm summer evenings a chance to stop and drink. If there's nowhere inspiring near you to walk then drive somewhere else and walk from there. Going for walks, years (or even decades) into a relationship, may take you not only down Pineview Avenue, but down memory lane as well. Indeed, if you make the same journey, retracing forgotten steps, those old passionate feelings will probably return.

20. It's in his kiss

If you believe a kiss is just a kiss, you've been conned.
If you want to recapture the closeness then pucker up.

The first step is to look after your lips. A daily slick of balm or flavoured gloss should keep your lips in perfect kissing condition. But avoid applying it just before going into action – slippery lips make sloppy kissers. If your lips are very chapped, try exfoliating them gently by covering them in balm and rubbing softly with a toothbrush. When you kiss, think about how you move your lips. Let them dance a little, playing with different degrees of friction and tension. Nibble, squeeze or trap your partner's bottom lip or tongue. Mess about and have fun.

Warm up and start slow. Changing speed mid-kiss should be like changing gear, smoothly and at appropriate times. Of course, sometimes we all like the thrill of going from 0 to 60 in three seconds, but not when we've just woken up.

Take a sip of champagne, hold it in your mouth and kiss your partner. Chilled bubbles on your lips and tongue introduce an extra dimension. For a less bling version, try a frozen cocktail. Why not recreate early tension by having furtive kissing sessions in semi-public places, like lifts and cinemas.

Kissing's not just for lips. Rediscover your partner's body: the insides of elbows, between the shoulder blades and the backs of knees - try to discover your partner's secret kiss-spots too.

21. Bloomin' marvellous

Want your love life to blossom? Say it with flowers.

Whatever your sentiment – striking, sensual, sanguine or sexy – there's a stem out there that will say it for you. You can't go wrong with roses. Velvety crimson petals exuding a heady fragrance. Reeks of seduction, doesn't it? Orchids, jasmine and lilies are also renowned for aphrodisiac scents. And flowers aren't just for women – rough and ready bouquets can appeal to men too.

To be really flash with flowers, you need to be au fait with the hand-tied bouquet. Just follow these six steps. It's worth the effort: Put the stems in a bowl of water and, using a sharp kitchen knife, remove all the side-shoots and leaves that will be underwater when the bouquet is in its vase.

Choose one striking flower and hold it upright in your left hand (or right hand, if you are left-handed). Add a few flowers. Make sure that the flower head is to the left and stem is to the right. As you add flowers, twist the flowers a quarter of a turn. Carry on adding flowers a few at a time and twisting. Twisting makes a spiral stem so the flowers stand upright. When you have run out of flowers, tie with ribbon at the place where you were holding them in your left (or right) hand. Wrap more ribbon round the stem if you want to or use raffia, wire or twine instead.

22. My favourite things

Birthdays, anniversaries, high days and holidays – what do you give the partner who's got everything?

How about giving presents according to traditional wedding anniversary themes? You don't have to be married. Use them to celebrate the anniversary of when you first met, first moved in together or first smiled at each other across a crowded train.

1st paper: any paper voucher makes a good gift.

2nd cotton: crisp, fresh, egyptian cotton bed sheets.

3rd leather: a gorgeous handbag or those shoes she really wants. For the guys, how about a wallet with a little something slipped inside?

4th linen: update bed linen, choose a gorgeous tablecloth and serve a memorable meal on it, or pledge to do all her laundry for a year?

5th wood: something personal (possibly hand crafted by you) will go down well – how about a small piece of furniture or a jewellery box?

6th iron: how about a new wrought iron bed?

7th copper: shiny pots or pans? Or perhaps plant a copper beech tree in the garden.

8th bronze: treat her to a fake tanning treatment, or better still, a holiday where she'll develop a real one.

9th china: a bone china dinner set. Alternatively, you could take him on a trip to the great wall.

10th aluminium: send your partner to the skies with a flying lesson.

23. Holiday romance

Use a vacation to inject a little romance into a jet-lagged love affair.

Whatever the weather, there's a perfect trip to recharge your love batteries. Spring is a time for renewal and growth; a perfect time for a reviving tour. Discover a new city together to learn new things about each other. Make the most of soaring temperatures and hot up your relationship. Miles of sandy beaches are perfect for holding hands and strolling.

Or how about an autumnal adventure? Pony trekking, quad biking or climbing will all leave you drenched in adrenaline, a key re-energising chemical. If your relationship's felt a bit frosty, warm up in a winter wonderland. There's nothing like cosying up in a comfy chalet before hitting the hot tub.

Holiday trouble for couples often has roots in different expectations. It pays to establish what each of you wants. Are you yearning for a peaceful escape or a daring adventure? Short trip or longer, more leisurely leave? Struggling to work out what you want? Think about your last holiday together. What worked well and what would you like to do differently this time? Compare your fantasy holidays and try to combine the best of both. If you're stuck, it's time to get the dice out. Write down your three top destinations each and number them one to six. Flip a coin to decide who gets to roll the dice, and… you've guessed it… the dice decides your final destination.

PING!

24. Undercover agents

Instead of rethreading the elastic into those greying boxer shorts, switch to sexy underwear and develop a sexy attitude.

At the start of relationships women tend to wear matching bras and briefs, lace body suits and slinky camisoles. And men make sure their underwear is clean. A few years down the line, we make the mistake of thinking we can get away with any old greying, fraying baggy granddad pants, because they're out of sight. No matter how long you've been together, knowing your partner is wearing underwear he or she looks fantastic in can give you both a little thrill.

Underwear represents the secret and intimate side of your relationship. But the right underwear can affect the way you look and feel in your outerwear too. When you choose underwear for yourself or your partner, think about what they'll wear it under and avoid an ugly visible knicker line. Tights are ugly. Nothing puts a damper on a relationship faster than a glimpse of flesh-coloured nylon wrinkling at the crotch. So whether you want to wear fishnets, lace tops or sheer, keep him in suspense with suspenders and hold up your relationship with held up hosiery – start stocking shocking stockings. Most women are wearing a wrong sized bra, which can be uncomfortable as well as unattractive. So go and be fitted professionally in a lingerie shop, (or why not have fun getting him to measure you up at home).

25. Stormy weather

Arguments happen in the best households, but they don't have to end in tears, tantrums or broken china.

Arguments are part of life. At best, they can spur you on to change aspects of your relationship or make you notice that your partner is unhappy. At worst, serious sulking or screaming sessions drag on for days, becoming aggressive power battles, and leaving you hurt and ground down. Disagreements can actually give your relationship a boost rather than lead to a bust up if you follow these rules.

Prevention is better than cure. If you always end up arguing about household bills, draw up a budget you both agree with. Discover what you're actually arguing about. Most arguments happen because of disagreements about work, money, sex or children. If you can resolve how you both feel about these topics, you'll live in harmony.

Forget about point scoring. Use words, not fists. If it gets violent, get help or get out. Likewise, insults, put-downs, critical comments, sarcasm and humiliation are all below the belt.

Compromise. If seeing your partner's socks on the floor makes you seethe, do a deal. Bargains like 'I'll wash up if you take the rubbish out' are less likely to cause fall outs than 'You lazy tosser. Clean up your own mess.' Say sorry when you hurt your partner. Forgive your partner for hurting you and forgive yourself for being unkind. Make up before you go to sleep.

26. Truly scentsational

Here's how to achieve the sweet smell of relationship success by following your nose.

We all produce chemicals that arouse the opposite sex. Male pheromones have a musky quality, so musk, an ingredient commonly used in perfumes, is a top turn on for women. And smelling lavender, doughnuts, liquorice, oriental spice and cola can all increase blood flow to the penis. If you don't fancy putting eau de doughnut in your oil burner, remember that the essential oils cinnamon, jasmine, musk, patchouli, rose, sandalwood and vanilla are the sexiest aromatherapy oils. They're believed to stimulate the release of neurochemicals, triggering sexual responses.

Don't just apply perfume to your wrists - other pulse points, like your navel, collarbone, behind your knees or on your ankle often get overlooked. Match your body lotion and perfume. In fact, layering, as the beauty pros call it, is the best way of making scent last. Use perfumed shower gel, then body lotion, before spritzing with eau de parfum (that's the concentrated one) and topping up during the day with eau de toilette.

Soft light and suggestive smells will get you both into a peaceful, loving mood so light a few scented candles. As a general rule, men like pine, sandalwood and frankincense, while women often prefer rose, lemon grass or ylang ylang. Play around and find something you both like.

27. Venn I fall in love

Stuck in a rut? Every discussion ending in an argument? Then it's time to return to the drawing board.

• Together draw two large overlapping circles. One circle represents each of you and the overlap represents things or qualities that are common to you both. You can use it to focus on any aspect of your lives from your finances to your social life. The stuff in the overlap of your Venn diagram is the glue that sticks you together.

• Spend about fifteen to twenty minutes filling in these Venn diagrams as comprehensively as possible. You can also include names of friends you have and don't have in common, places, TV programmes, books, films, newspapers even politics. The more wide-ranging and specific you can be the better.

• Share and compare. Time for some home truths. Some things will be self-evident while other items will need to be qualified.

• Look at the overlap and brainstorm ways of focusing on what you've got in common. If you both hate washing up, perhaps it's time to buy a dishwasher.

• Again using words in the overlap, try to deconstruct mutual interests. What is it about darts you both find so attractive? Is it being competitive, being members of a team, the banter in the pub, or representing the pub in other locals? This sort of questioning generates ideas for other shared interests.

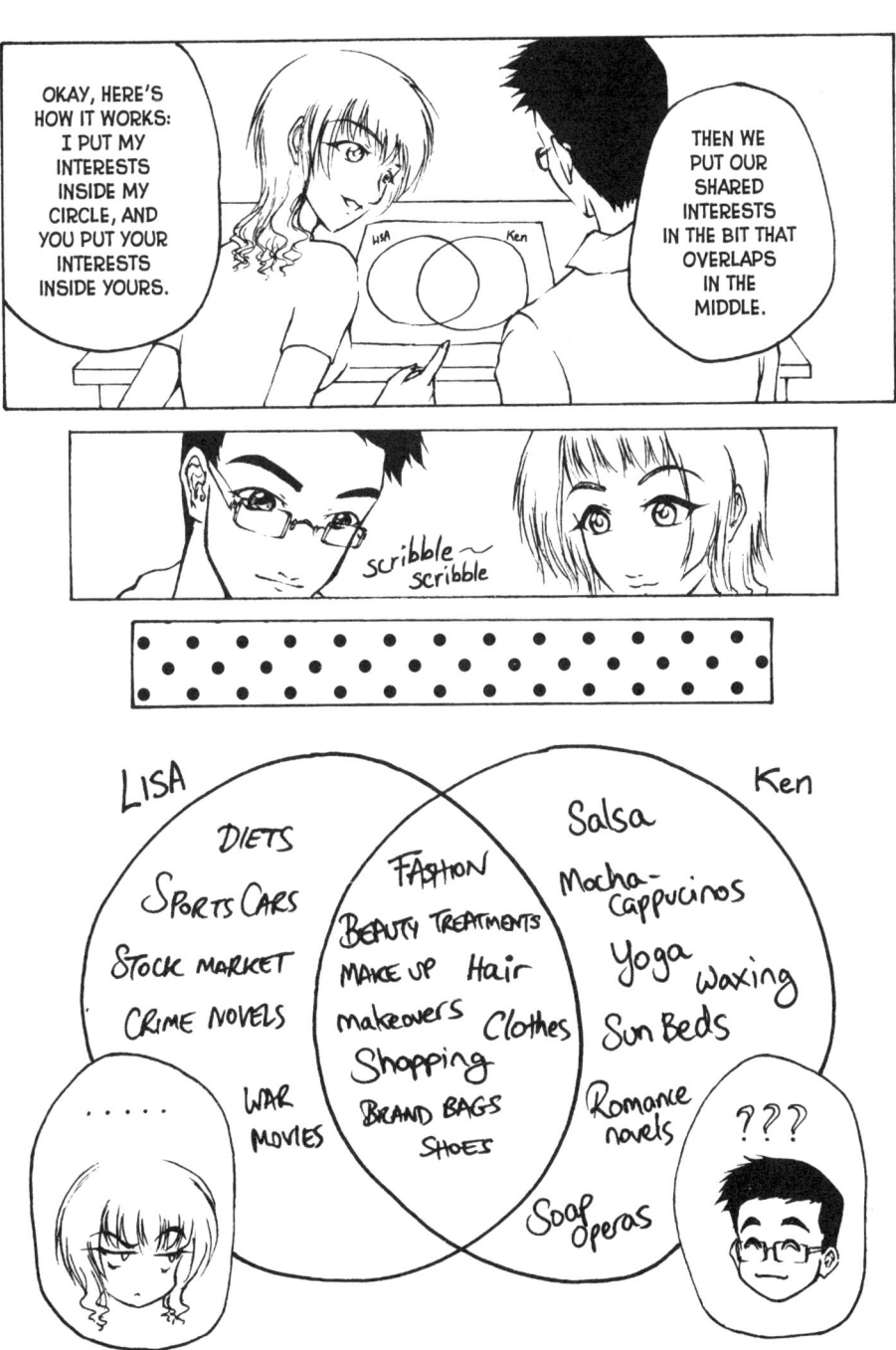

28. Jealous guy

Banishing jealous feelings is bound to revitalise your relationship. Recognise them and act.

Jealousy's a funny emotion. The object of your desire wanting you all to him or herself can be strangely seductive, for a little while. But this soon wears off and relentless jealousy grates.

Jealous partners make us feel like caged lovebirds: trapped and aching to fly away at the earliest opportunity. Maybe you've been censoring conversations, seeing friends less or are afraid of provoking a watchful partner into one of her rages. Jealous lovers are usually deeply insecure. But take heart. Once you understand that their possessiveness isn't a sign of your desirability but comes from a need to be loved and to control, you can tame the feral green-eyed monster.

Let's be honest. Window shopping, eye candy, whatever you want to call it – everyone looks at other people sometimes. Most of us are just discreet enough not to get caught. If you and your partner can agree on a look but don't touch rule, there isn't any need to feel threatened. If you can go one further, and point out other people your partner will probably fancy, what relationship expert Leil Lowndes calls giving 'guilt free snacks', the green-eyed monster will turn into a green-eyed house pet. In Leil's words, 'If he has his guilt free gander, you will have a much happier goose.'

29. Bewitched...

Flirting with the milkman? Exchanging glances with your guitar teacher?

A frisson of safe excitement can brighten office life and casual flirting makes a mundane journey or chore a lot more enjoyable. The danger is located at home. Almost imperceptibly the passion and sparkle that once existed in your domestic life can leak away like water from a punctured paddling pool. The trick is to find ways to keep the flame of passion alight with your partner. How to avoid temptation:

• Build self-esteem: people often have affairs to feel better about themselves. Pulling a new partner makes you feel successful at something and desirable again. But only in the short term.

• Face problems when they arise: affairs can be a way of avoiding trouble at home. Dealing with the root of small problems as they arise prevents a lot of bother later.

• Cultivate emotional intimacy: you both need to say how you feel to understand each other's moods and outbursts. If things feel fiery, take time out to cuddle up.

Affairs are fun because they are furtive and clandestine. Why not have an affair with your partner? Meet in a bar and pretend not to know each other. Watch other men flirt with her, before chatting her up. Wink at him across a crowded train carriage. Phone him at work and whisper a come-on. Or send saucy emails.

30. Saying sorry

Some of us would rather face a firing squad than admit we're wrong. If the 's' word sticks in your throat, it's time to bite the bullet.

The best time to say sorry is as soon as you notice that you've hurt your partner. Of course it's incredibly difficult to break mid-argument and offer an apology. Especially if you're winning. If you can express regret after, or even during, an argument, great. On the other hand, if you calm down a bit you won't sound insincere.

Saying sorry is useless unless your partner knows why you're apologising. You need to acknowledge what you've done wrong. Be specific, no matter how much it makes you squirm. Sarcasm or a half-hearted apology, like 'You know I didn't mean it' or 'You know I'm not all bad', is worse than no apology at all because your partner will probably feel you are being disingenuous.

Apologies need to be accepted with grace and good will, rather than as ammunition for mud slinging and accusation.

Words are sometimes enough, but actions usually speak louder. Gifts can make your partner feel pressurised or even blackmailed into accepting your apology before he's ready. Far better to follow your verbal apology with action related to your transgression. If your partner's cross because you never wash up, get the rubber gloves on or buy a dishwasher. If your girlfriend's upset after finding your stash of Horny Housewife, cancel the subscription. Whatever you've done, don't apologise only to commit the same sin again.

31. Hike up the heartbeat

Daredevil dates that make your partner's heart beat faster will make you irresistible.

Thirty years ago, a couple of psychologists wrote a paper entitled 'Some evidence for heightened sexual attraction under conditions of high anxiety'. They asked a group of guys to cross one of two bridges. The first was a scarily shaky suspension bridge far above a canyon; the other was a solid bridge over a small brook.

After crossing the bridge, each man was met by a beautiful researcher. She asked him to complete a short questionnaire, in which he had to categorise some fairly vague pictures of people. She then gave the guy her phone number. 'Call me,' she said, 'if there's anything you want to ask about the study.' The guys who crossed the wobbly bridge were much more likely to call, and found more sexy themes in the pictures they were shown after crossing the bridge. Crossing the suspension bridge gave them an adrenaline surge, so when they saw the beautiful woman, the men confused their increased heart rates with sexual arousal. Do something scary with your beloved, and make it work for you.

The bad news is that the converse works, too. If you and your partner are supremely bored, sooner or later she'll start to think of you as dramatically boring. So go on a different sort of date such as paragliding, bunjee jumping or white water rafting.

32. Our house

Our homes affect how we feel about our relationships. If your home is not a sanctuary then you might find your relationship suffering.

Often treasures from our past anchor us there preventing us from concentrating on what matters now. If the thought of parting with possessions you've outgrown depresses you, at least sell, donate or throw away reminders of previous relationships.

When one partner moves into a home the other already owns or rents, it's vital to make space. Your relationship will feel a lot more equal if you go through the flat, clearing out old books and CDs, and 'rationalising' collections of whatever you own that says 'this is my house', whether it be china pigs or old issues of Computer Weekly.

Some couples work so hard climbing the property ladder that it destroys their lives and relationship. But if you think it's time to move out and move on muse on these with your beloved:

• What does this home stop us doing?
• What was it that first attracted us to this home?

   • How have our needs and circumstances changed since?
   • Has the area changed: is it a better or worse place than it was?
   • Could we convert the house and change its use?
   • What would we miss if we moved?
   • If we replaced this house with an inexpensive flat, how would we spend the windfall?

I GUESS IF I'M STICKING WITH BEN, I OUGHT TO HAVE A CLEAROUT.

I'VE NEVER REALLY MADE ROOM IN MY LIFE FOR JUST ONE MAN BEFORE... BUT BEN'S SO GORGEOUS, HE'S WORTH IT.

~dHm dhmmm dd2
Hmmhm dy~

RUMMAGE... RUMMAGE...

AH, DYLAN... YOU WERE LOTS OF FUN.

Magician's Kit

HM!! CHRIS!! THOSE WERE THE DAYS.

BEST OF 1996
Noah's Chart Toppers!

...MICHAEL. YES... BIG EGO. NOT SO BIG DOWN BELOW.

STUD MUFFIN

33. April in Paris

Long-haul lovers know mini-breaks make a massive difference.

Mini-breaks are a chance to live life away from the mundane grind and put some sparkle back in your relationship. Where you go doesn't matter, it's what you do there that counts. Forget location and instead plan around an activity your partner will delight in.

When your chocoholic chap realises you've taken him to Belgium for a handmade truffle demonstration, or your wife realises you've travelled miles to see her favourite comedian, it all falls into place. He or she will feel understood, loved and cherished.

If you can keep your break secret from your partner and make it a surprise, you're onto a winner. If you can't collect your partner, you could send a taxi or a mysterious email saying 'Meet me at the airport at 7pm', which will make your beloved's heart beat faster.

If money is tight, spend most of it on your activity and scrimp on the accommodation. A bottle of bubbly, some romantic tealights, a vase of flowers and your own bedsheets can turn an average room in a cheap B&B into a boudoir. We're not saying four poster beds, champagne and roses don't help, they're just optional extras. Think of them as garnish.

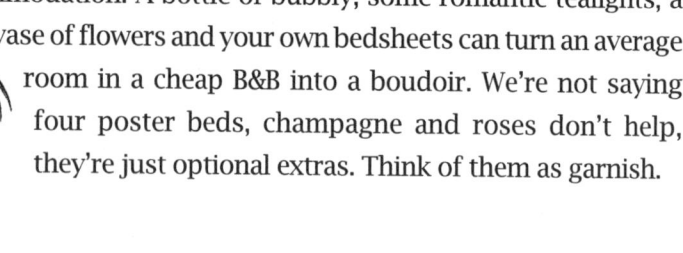

34. Wonderful tonight

Give your old flame first-date butterflies with a makeover that brings out the best in both of you.

Take advantage of the free personal shopper service offered by many department stores. Explain that you want a look to make your long-term lover weak at the knees. The shopper should then bring you a selection of styles to suit your size, frame, personality and budget. It's up to you whether you love it or leave it.

There's no quicker way to change your partner's reaction from ho-hum to wow than by blowing your budget at the hairdresser. While we're talking about hair, make sure you shave, pluck, wax and bleach where needed too. Get that come hither look by plucking your eyebrows into shape. Yes, even men. If you haven't got time to do full eye make-up, a whisk of mascara can transform your look, drawing attention to your eyes. Many metrosexual men already know mascara also comes in clear.

Eyes may be the windows of the soul, but when you reach out to touch your partner, how often is it with silky smooth hands rather than ones chapped and worn by washing up, gardening or typing? A callused caress isn't very sexy. If you usually work with your hands, it's time to get to work on them. Smooth rough hands by mixing some sea salt with olive oil and rubbing it all over them. A few strokes with a nail buffer means you can leave nails naked, if you haven't time to polish up your act with varnish.

35. Friendly advice

Time to clear out your address book as you would old clothes.

Fill your lives with people you admire, who inspire you and who will support you. Stick with these friends:

- Couples where you like and get on with both partners equally.
- Couples in relationships where no one is the boss.
- Couples who are great listeners, who seem interested in you.
- Positive people who are prepared to try new things.
- People who share your sense of humour and fun.
- People who are great mixers, who get on with your family and other friends, and who you are happy to see in any company.
- People you can talk to when you or they are unhappy.
- People who reciprocate hospitality.
- People who don't take sides in one of your fall-outs.

Banish these types:

- People who have envious pops about you and your life.
- Couples and individuals who have to dominate anything from conversation to restaurant choices.
- Bloodsuckers: people affected with contagious forms of negativity.
- Guilt-inducing 'friends' unable to accept that you can't always drop everything and have a meal with them at two hours' notice

36. Love and marriage

Arranging your own special day gives your relationship a boost that lasts.

A marriage certificate may just be a piece of paper, but the emotional investments, legal ties and public declarations make it your most important possession. Publicly promising to stay with your partner forever profoundly changes your relationship. Making or renewing vows buttresses previous promises. Marriage is a chance to stop and think about what we want for our relationships and what we need to get there.

Heard that weddings are stressful and strain relationships? Not if you ignore the propaganda peddled by the wedding industry. Instead, work together to create a day as personal and individual as your relationship. A local art college can put you in touch with centres where you can design your own wedding rings. Or get a shop-bought ring and have it inscribed with a secret or personal message. In most countries you can personalise the script, add your own rituals to more traditional ones or make it up completely. You may need a civil ceremony as well to cover all the legal bits.

There's no reason why you and your partner can't cherry pick the best bits of the wedding ceremony to create an unforgettable commitment ceremony. Commitment doesn't have to be legal to be powerful or life changing. Nevertheless, some couples do include legally binding arrangements, like wills or property ownership.

37. Special days

Sometimes you need to pull all the stops out and have a life-changing day.

Perhaps you're both sick of the same routine? Boyfriend having a hard time at work? Need to make your 25th valentine's day as dynamic as the first? Just moved house? Or the best reason of all: just because.

Book the best suite in a nearby hotel. Waking up in a mahogany four poster will make the most jaded couple feel like royalty. It's the perfect start to a wonderful day out of life. Use this day to do something totally different.

Spend the morning at the races or arrange a private guided tour of a favourite gallery or museum followed by lunch. After a little light window shopping or a romantic stroll, toast each other over a champagne afternoon tea with sandwiches, scones and cake.

Early evening is happy hour so dress up and order classy Cosmopolitans or Bellinis. Afterwards take in a play or show, or even go to the cinema if that's what you prefer – just make sure you book the best seats in the house.

Give your evening meal the film star treatment. Write a love letter or card and ask the waiter to hide it in your partner's menu. Present him with a small gift between the main course and dessert. After you've eaten, go for a sunset stroll.

38. Domestic detox

Review your chores and renew your romance.

At the beginning of your relationship did you sit down and decide who was going to take out the dustbin every Wednesday evening? Vacuum the lounge? Cook Sunday dinner? Did you ever agree that one or other of you would do the bulk of the long-distance car journeys or always sort out the tickets for airline bookings? Of course you didn't. Yet in most relationships, we find ourselves committed to being the only person doing a particular task. But why should one particular person be lumbered with changing the cat litter tray or making sure that the household doesn't run out of toilet paper and toothpaste? Many couples have come to realise that cooking or even tidying up hardly feels like a chore when the two of you are tackling it together.

In a lot of long-term partnerships, one or other member suffers from what we call 'victim of your own success syndrome'. One partner always reads maps or does the big drives because she is better at it than he is. Of course she is: she's put in the mileage. But if you share the job around, his second best can easily become joint equal. When a lover's self-esteem is built on being the sole role-holder, he might find it difficult to let go. When your partner has a go at what is traditionally your job, avoid being critical or sniping if at first they don't measure up – neither did you when you first started.

39. Cheap thrills

You don't have to blow a fortune to blow the cobwebs out of your relationship.

Here are seven cheap and cheerful dates:
• Have a home cinema night. Rent the first film you watched together, make mountains of microwave popcorn and turn your sofa into the back row.
• Eat at home but go out afterwards for desserts and coffee in a swanky restaurant.
• Rendezvous in an exclusive hotel. You don't need to book a room, just put on your finery and people watch in the lounge with a drink.
• Theatre matinees are often as little as half price so take the afternoon off work and take in a show together.
• Many artists and crafts people have open days and other free events in their studios. Gather inspiration or maybe even buy some art.
• Serve breakfast in bed with a themed twist. For a French breakfast, put on some accordion music and serve hot coffee and pain au chocolat. French maid's outfits and moustaches optional.
• Drop in on an open mic night at a comedy club. As this is where new acts cut their teeth, you won't see any famous faces, but what a thrill to see someone before they are famous.

40. Reach out and touch

When did you last reach out and touch the person you love?

Words are great, but your fingers can reach places language never can. The finest touching is a sensual conversation. When you next touch your partner, wait for a reply before touching further. So if you stroke her cheek, wait until she squeezes your arm before running your finger over her eyebrows. Between people who are attracted to each other, just brushing fingertips can send shock waves. Try making little circles with your fingertips on your partner's palm or inner elbow, or the nape of his neck. Do this at mundane times, like waiting for a bus, then next time your partner is waiting for a bus without you, he'll realise that it's just not as much fun as when you're there. A cunning piece of prestidigitation.

When non-sexual touch is neglected, we become belligerent and dejected. But after prolonged touching, the hypothalamic area of the brain, which controls the fight or flight response, slows down and your body's natural euphoria-inducing chemicals – endorphins – soar, while the stress hormone cortisol dips. When you're being touched by your beloved, your mind associates all these good feelings with them, leaving you feeling loved up and secure. If you're going through a difficult time, try to keep a hand or another part of your body in contact with your beloved. It will help you feel united.

41. Getting it right

How do you get your lover to love you the way you want to be loved?

The person who can tell their lover that they want to be touched differently from the way they've been touched a million times before is pretty rare. But there are ways to ask without embarrassing yourself and mortifying your lover. Using phrases starting with 'Why don't you...', 'You never...' or 'That doesn't...' will cause offence and your partner will get defensive...and whining is deeply unattractive. Instead follow these steps:

• Be an appreciative lover. Do it with body language. Do it loudly. Spell it out. They should finish every session assured that you're blissfully happy. Your 'win' is that besides being a lovely person you're also gearing them up for moving your sex life on to greater heights.

• Next, modify the technique by focusing on the positive. For instance, 'I love the way you do that, especially when you go slowly/ quickly/hang off the headboard while you're doing it.' Use discretion and be specific if possible. Use your hands to gently direct the action the way you want it.

• Now you can suggest doing it differently. Do it lightly, with grace, not as if your entire sexual happiness depends on it (remember they can't fail). Say that you've read about something you'd like to try in a book and ask if they would oblige...

42. Learn the art of kaizen

Kaizen is a Japanese concept that means, 'Small changes, big differences.' It can revolutionise your love life.

Promise yourself that the next time you make love you will, as far as possible, work on the rule of difference – if you always start with kissing, try flipping your lover over and massaging their shoulders instead; if you prefer to be on top, then lie on your back. You'll feel resistance, as your instincts will be to follow the same old pattern, but fight it: absolutely nothing is more ruinous to your love life than doing things more or less the same way more or less all the time. Both of you need to try to make sex just a little bit different from the last time or the half a dozen times before that.

Men often wish that their partner would initiate sex more, but what they really mean is initiate sex when they vaguely fancy it. Not, of course, when they're immersed in the cricket, which would be annoying. And annoyed is what your girlfriend feels when you leap on her while she's sorting laundry. Men are generally terrific at bouncing back from rejection because most tend to get lots of practice in adolescence, and they're also willing to put up with their partner taking a moment to get on their sexual wavelength but women take that original hesitation on your part as outright rejection and turn away. Ask her to surprise you just once in the upcoming month but don't pressurise.

"SMALL CHANGES, BIG DIFFERENCE". KAIZEN. AND IT'S SUPPOSED TO HELP KEEP RELATIONSHIPS FRESH.

INTERESTING. I'VE NEVER HEARD OF THAT TERM BEFORE.

I'M TRYING TO APPLY THAT LOGIC WITH BEN AT THE MOMENT - HE'S SUCH A CATCH!

BUT SOMETIMES IT'S DIFFICULT TO COME UP WITH NEW IDEAS, PARTICULARLY IN THE BEDROOM.

OH, I WOULD NEVER HAVE THAT PROBLEM.

HUH? WHY?

BECAUSE I HAVE 32 DIFFERENT SEX TOYS, REMEMBER?

OH! WOULD YOU LIKE TO BORROW-

NO!! BORROWING IS JUST... WRONG!!

43. What's your LQ score?

Imagine you're in the Mastermind chair and your specialist subject is your lover. What would be your love quotient (LQ) score?

Broadly speaking, to successfully love the person we're with we need to understand what they need to feel loved. To keep their love we must give them what they need as far as possible. Loads of couples are having indifferent or absolutely no sex, not because they don't spark off each other but because they haven't felt loved by their partner for years. When your lover's feeling insecure, stressed or worried, how do you make them feel safe and reassured? Does it work? If not, do you know what would? If yes, why do you withhold it from them? Do you like to play mean just for the hell of it? It might seem to work and it might keep you the 'superior' partner, but the price is high. Your partner won't be able to trust you and that sort of trust is near enough essential to keep sex hot between you when the first thrill has gone.

Would your lover rather have a romantic meal or a wild night out on the town as a prelude to sex? Do you occasionally indulge them, even if you'd rather do something else? Emotionally we have to be given chocolates at least some of the time or we start to shut off from our partner and get tempted by someone who appears to offer Milk Tray on demand. If you're with someone for whom chocolate equals love, all the roses in the world won't fix your relationship or help you get good sex.

44. Sleep is the new sex – honest!

I know a woman who tried to convince her lover that the really happening people were giving up sex in favour of sleep.

Competitive tiredness between couples is a relatively new phenomenon and one result of both partners being strung out with exhaustion is no nookie. It's not of course the end of a relationship if you go some time with a lacklustre or indeed non-existent love life. But keep using tiredness as an excuse and before you know it, total inertia has set in.

Having sex when you're tired can start off indifferently and get a whole lot better. And even if it doesn't indifferent sex is better than no sex. Make definite dates when you're going to do it. Make sex that day your priority. See it as a red-letter event.

Reorganising your workloads can help. Think of all your household chores and work out who does more around the home. Make sure you put everything on the list from ironing and grocery shopping to doing the DIY. This exercise can be an eye-opener for couples that think they have a pretty equal relationship. If it's not so equal, you have to take steps to delegate or equalise your workload, or your sex life is unlikely to get back to normal any time soon.

You might be reading this and thinking, 'I'm the major breadwinner, I work my butt off and can't do vacuuming and ironing, too.' But you'll have to find some compromise for the sake of your relationship.

ARE YOU SURE YOU REALLY DON'T WANT TO COME TO THE CLUB WITH US?

YUP. I'M WAITING FOR LISA TO COME HOME.

BUT IT'S YOUR FAVOURITE DJ PLAYING TONIGHT, AND WEDNESDAY NIGHT HAS HALF PRICE COCKTAILS!

YES, BUT WEDNESDAY NIGHT IS ALSO... BUSINESS TIME.

WHAT?!

LISA AND I HAVE SUCH BUSY SCHEDULES, WE'VE DECIDED WE SHOULD *DO IT* ON WEDNESDAYS IF WE'RE BOTH IN. SO, I'D BETTER BE IN, OR I'LL MISS MY SLOT.

SO CLINICAL... LIKE A DOCTOR'S APPOINTMENT.

45. Coming over all touchy-feely

Learn to express sensuality with your whole body.

Showering together is one of those things we do at the beginning of a relationship that tails off with age and familiarity. Give your lover a surprise this week. Wait until it's good and steamy in there. Strip off, step in and start soaping them down. Note for women: put on some gorgeous wispy underwear and step into the shower with him when he's not expecting it. The feel (and the look!) of the wet fabric plastered against your slick body and the rush he'll get from pushing it aside to get at you should make for a different kind of experience.

Look for different ways to surprise each other with unexpected sensations:

* Wear something different from the norm. If you sleep naked, try silk pyjama bottoms. If you always wear a nightdress, change to a simple white cotton brief and vest set.

* Take an ice cube and rub it over your lover's bare back or nipples while you're making love until it melts.

* Ladies: get your man to lie on his front, straddle him from behind and whisper in his ear that he's going to help you to come. Then apply oil on his back and your body and start slithering up and down on him. What's more likely to make your lover mad for you than letting him know he's driving you mad with lust?

46. Something for the weekend

Here are some ideas for solving two common relationship problems during a typical two-day break. Use them as a model to write out your own 'prescription for love'.

If you're turning into 'just friends' and need to become lovers again: **Day 1.** Pretend that you are new lovers who aren't ready to move on to the sexual stage of a relationship. Be a little shy and take time with your appearance. Be determined to find them deeply endearing, no matter how much they were irritating you yesterday.

Day 2. Resolve to do something you'll never forget. Create new, shared, sexual memories that will stay with both of you when you get home and fuel desire when the rut beckons again. Move mirrors in your hotel room so that you can see yourselves while you have sex. Throw your lover against a wall in a tiny cobbled street. Slip away from the lights and make love on the beach.

If your love life is predictable:

Day 1. Create intimacy. Spend a couple of hours bathing, showering and massaging each other before dinner. Don't rush into sex. Rediscover each other. Hold hands. Maintain eye contact as much as possible. Spend time talking about your feelings about work, family, friends and your relationship. Your aim is to make your lover feel cherished and 'listened to'.

Day 2. Break the patterns. Each write three things you'd like to try on a piece of paper. Take turns to fulfil each other's wishes.

47. In out, in out

Turn the simple breathing action into a way to heighten sexual pleasure and get closer to your partner. Try the exercises below.

The **'complete'** breath. Draw breath in, hold the breath in your lungs, exhale and then pause before breathing again. Practice this and then breathe in for one count, hold for four counts, breathe out for two counts and pause. Repeat this until it comes naturally.

Focusing on lurve. A good basis for a mini-meditation session before you make love. Concentrate on taking in energy in with each inward breath and, with each outward breath, bringing your concentration to bear on how you're feeling right here, right now.

Breathing in Unison. This simple breathing exercise is a quick way to improve communication. Try it once a day, in bed or out, clothed or not. Hold onto each other and regulate your breaths. Let thoughts drift away as they float into your mind. Just be with each other. Lie in bed, 'spooned' around one another, and simply breathe in unison.

Heart breathing. Sit on your bed in a comfortable position facing each other. Place your hands flat on your chest between your breasts. Close your eyes. Now breathe as in 'The complete breath' above. Imagine you're drawing love in with each breath and, while holding it in your lungs, feel it nourishing your body and spirit. Finally, when you breathe out imagine your breath leaving your body as a wave of love rolling over and around your partner. Open your eyes and look at your partner while you breathe together.

48. Just say 'no'

There's saying 'no' and there's saying 'no' nicely. Two very different things.

Every relationship has times when sex is off the cards. This can hurt your relationship. If your partner approaches you and you feel ambivalent about having sex, go along with it for a while and try to get yourself in the mood (with their help, of course). If, however, you fail to rise onto that wave of lust, all you can do is gaze into their eyes tenderly and say, 'Sorry, it isn't working for me tonight, but I promise that tomorrow we'll do the deed.' Sex therapists agree that rejection is easier to take if there's a definite date set for a rematch.

But what if you know that tomorrow you're not going to want to have sex either? Decide on a time when you're going to get physical and then do all you can to get yourself in the mood, such as a bath, delicious food, candles or a chat. Don't expect mind-bending lust – mildly being up for it is good enough. Being physically close without having penetrative sex can eventually kick start your libido.

If you really can't be bothered to do all you can to get yourself and your partner in the mood for sex then you're a rotten lover. Your lover is almost certain to get depressed and unconfident – both traits are hell to live with and unlikely to endear them to you. Keeping your sex life alive is important for your mental health and theirs.

49. Developing sexual mystique

Yes, it's possible. Even if you've shared a bathroom for years.

❝Male and female are different,' says relationship counsellor Paula Hall. 'And we've known since the sixties that if a couple want a stable relationship, it's worth working at maintaining that difference. She points out that studies by psychologists have already picked up on the dangers of becoming too alike. 'We call it "enmeshment" when couples become too similar,' says Hall. 'It's been known for a long time that it can have a detrimental impact on desire.'

Keep interested in life, stay full of vim and brio for other projects, remain engaged with people outside of your relationship and be passionate about the world. Then bring that energy home and translate it into passion for each other. Talk about your lives with such enthusiasm that your partner can't help get a kick out of your enthusiasm, charm, intelligence and all-round top-quality personality.

Rule 1. All couples fall into a pattern of 'we don't do that'. But if you fancy doing something different, suggest it anyway. Don't argue if they say 'no'. The point has been made. You've reinforced in both your minds that you're different individuals. Rule 2. Support your partner as much as possible when they're trying to be an individual. Rule 3. Be yourself. Don't take on his interests and hobbies unless they genuinely interest you, too. Be equal but not the same.

50. Dealing with burnout

That's what we call it when your relationship is a mess and you just don't care.

If too many people want a bit of you you need to set boundaries and cut down on commitments. People who don't set boundaries often end up playing out their frustrations in the bedroom. This is equally true for the woman who withdraws sex as the man who, although he wants sex, isn't affectionate because he feels overburdened with responsibility. When you're too tired for sex or to give your partner what they need to feel good, the answer is to spend time cutting loose from all commitment. Time alone gives you a sense of balance and renewal, which can give you more energy.

If you're bored with life you need to rediscover your passion and revel in pleasure. You may well be having a mid-life crisis – even if you're only 25. Tell your partner, honestly, what's wrong. Then you can negotiate more time for yourself, more holidays together. Whatever it takes to get more pleasure into your life, because pleasure is the only cure for burnout. Your partner might not like some of your ideas but if yours is a good healthy relationship then they'll live with whatever it takes to return you to the happy love bunny you were of yore. Unless, of course, it threatens them or the relationship, in which case you don't have a healthy relationship and you need more help than is on offer here.

51. Pressure – it's not a dirty word

For times when you want to feast on a banquet of love, there is massage.

First, select your oil. Create your own blend by adding eight to ten drops of oil (or a mixture of oils) to three dessertspoons of a base oil such as almond. Good oils for sensual massage are geranium, which is uplifting and grounding; lavender, which is relaxing and soothing; sandalwood, which is warming and encouraging; and ylang ylang, which is sensual and erotic.

Choose a warm, comfortable place in your home. Put on some gentle music and lower the lights. Take some oil and warm it between your palms. Then start working it into your partner's back, using firm gliding strokes. The secret of applying pressure is to channel the strength of your body through the balls of your thumbs. Lean into your lover's body but apply pressure only to the meaty parts of the body (but not the belly). Don't apply pressure on hard bony areas.

Alternate sweeping movements with gentle pressure across the back, buttocks and the back of legs. Use long strokes along the arms and gently pull at each finger in turn. Try different pressures. Concentrate on your lover's body and giving pleasure. Ask for a little feedback., but don't talk too much. Allow your partner to relax.

Ask your partner to turn over. Holding their head steady with your knees and massaging their face is particularly relaxing. Don't directly touch their genitals – the oils may irritate sensitive areas.

52. The least you need to do...

...to keep your relationship minty fresh.

Rule 1: Daily...Carve out fifteen minutes of every day to talk. Go to bed before your usual time or get up earlier and have a coffee together so you can touch base. Kiss each other every morning before you get out of bed. Take the time for a swift cuddle. Breathe deeply. Hold tight. Do the same at night. Never take your physical intimacy for granted. You found each other – pretty amazing – so acknowledge it.

Rule 2: Weekly...Go out with each other. Once a fortnight is the bare minimum. According to the experts, this is the most important thing you can do. Spending too long sloping around the same house does something to a couple's sexual interest in each other and what it does generally isn't good. So get out, preferably after making some small effort to tart yourself up so you're visually pleasing to your partner. Let them see why they bothered with you in the first place.

Rule 3: Monthly...Go for a mini-adventure – shared memories cement your relationship. It really doesn't matter what it is, as long as it's not your usual 'date'. You see your partner coping with new environments and new skills and that keeps you interested in them. And them in you. Simple.

Copyright © Infinite Ideas Ltd (text)
and Sweatdrop Studios (illustrations), 2008

The right of the writers and illustrator to be identified as
the authors of this book has been asserted in accordance
with the Copyright, Designs and Patents Act 1988.

First published in 2008 by
Infinite Ideas Limited
36 St Giles
Oxford, OX1 3LD
United Kingdom
www.infideas.com

A CIP catalogue record for this book is available from the British Library
ISBN 978-1-905940-78-3

Brand and product names are trademarks or registered
trademarks of their respective owners.

Cover design by Cylinder, illustration by Sonia Leong
Text design and typesetting by Cylinder
Printed in India

Infinite Ideas would like to thank Peter Cross, Sabina Dosani, Lisa
Helmanis and Elisabeth Wilson for their contributions to this book.